THE FRUIT OF THE SPIRIT

GROWING TO BE LIKE JESUS

Marcus J. Ford
Illustrated by Darrien Lindsey

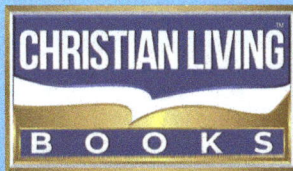

CHRISTIAN LIVING
B O O K S

Christian Living Books, Inc.
We bring your dreams to fruition.
ChristianLivingBooks.com

ISBN 9781562295950

Books may be purchased in bulk at special discounts for churches, schools, sales promotions, corporate gifts, fund-raising, or educational purposes. Special Editions can also be created to specifications. For details, contact the Special Sales Department at info@christianlivingbooks.com.

Introduction

Welcome to the wonderful garden of the Holy Spirit! In this special place, we'll learn about the amazing fruit that God grows in our hearts when we follow Jesus—love, joy, peace, patience, kindness, goodness, faithfulness, gentleness, and self-control. They show everyone what God's love looks like!

As we explore each of these fruits, we'll discover how Jesus displayed them perfectly in His life on earth. But the best part is that Jesus gives us the power to grow it in our own lives!

Let's explore how these special qualities can change our lives and the lives of those around us, making the world a brighter and happier place. So, get ready to grow in God's love and learn how to be more like Jesus every day!

Love

Love is a special gift from God that fills our hearts and helps us care for others. The strawberry shows love by using its leaves to make shade for the smaller, hot raspberry. Just like the strawberry helps the raspberry feel better, God wants us to help others and show them His love.

The Bible says, "Dear friends, let us continue to love one another, for love comes from God" (1 John 4:7). That means when we are loving and kind, even when it's hard, we are being just like God!

Jesus showed us what perfect love looks like. He was always kind, sharing, and forgiving, even to people who weren't nice to Him. He even gave His life to save us because He loves us so much!

We can show love in lots of ways – by sharing our toys, giving hugs, helping with chores, and telling others about Jesus. Every time we choose love, we make God smile and help others see how wonderful He is.

Love is like a beautiful flower that keeps growing. The more we love God and others, the more our hearts will be filled with His love. It's not always easy, but with God's help, we can love even when people aren't kind to us or when we don't feel like it.

One great way to practice love is by praying for others, even those who have hurt us. We can ask God to bless them and help them know His love. Another way is by looking for opportunities to serve, like making a card for a sick friend, sharing our snack with someone who forgot theirs, or inviting a new kid to play.

As we show love, we'll discover the joy that comes from putting others first and making them feel valued. We'll be shining God's light and planting seeds of kindness that He can grow into something beautiful.

So, let's ask God to fill us with His love each day and help us share it freely. May our lives be a lovely garden that points others to Jesus!

Love is an action word,
so you gave us Your Son.
You demonstrate that
by leaving 99 for the one.

You're a Good Father,
it is who You are.
Your Love is near
and is never far.

We can always call on You
Your Love draws us in close.
When trouble comes,
we count on You most.

My God sent His Son
down just for me,
Because of Your Love,
I will live for eternity.

To Love like Your Son
is true success.
I'll be obedient to You
and You'll handle the rest.

Joy

Joy is the wonderful feeling we have when we trust God. Look at that banana dancing and smiling, even though it's a rainy day. Happiness may be based on what we have or what's going on around us, but the fruit of joy comes from having Jesus in our hearts no matter what.

God wants us to have joy, not just when things are good, but all the time. In the Bible, Paul says, "Always be full of joy in the Lord. I say it again—rejoice" (Philippians 4:4). He was telling us to choose joy and keep smiling because of Jesus!

One way to have more joy is to count our blessings each day. We can thank God for our family, friends, food, toys, and all the amazing things He's given us. Another way is to spread joy to others by being kind, sharing, and telling them about Jesus.

As we choose joy, we'll feel God's happiness bubbling up inside like a big balloon. We'll smile more and help others smile too. Joy is contagious – the more we have it, the more it spreads!

Sometimes, it can be hard to be joyful, especially when life is difficult, or people are unkind. But even in those tough times, we can ask God to help us find a reason to smile. Maybe it's a funny joke, a beautiful flower, or a simple "I love you" from Mom or Dad.

Another great way to practice joy is by singing and dancing! Play your favorite praise songs or gospel music and let the joy of the Lord move you. Sing about how amazing God is and how much He loves you. Dance like that joyful banana in the rain, celebrating all that Jesus has done for you.

As you praise God with a thankful heart, you'll be reminded that no matter what happens, you always have a reason to rejoice because you belong to Jesus. And as others see your joy shining through, they'll want to know the secret behind your smile – the incredible love of God!

So, let's ask God to fill us with His joy every single day and help us spread it around like confetti.

Joy is not just a feeling
but the fruit from Christ.
We choose our feelings,
to be happy, mad, or nice.

Everyone wants to be happy,
but the Joy of the Lord is key.
For any situation that you are in,
Joy should always run deep.

I say choose Joy over happiness
because happiness can change.
But with Joy in your heart,
you always remain the same.

Find Joy in your life,
and you will be proud.
Because if we choose our own desires
we may fall down to the ground.

Peace

Peace is feeling calm and safe because we trust God. See the pineapple resting peacefully in the hammock? He's not worried about anything because He knows God is taking care of him.

Sometimes life feels scary or mixed up, but God promises to give us peace when we pray and remember He's in charge. The Bible says, "Don't worry about anything; instead, pray about everything... Then you will experience God's peace, which exceeds anything we can understand" (Philippians 4:6-7).

When Jesus was on a boat in a big storm, He was so peaceful that He fell asleep! His friends were afraid and woke Him up. Jesus told the wind and waves to be still, and everything became calm (Mark 4:39). He showed us that we can have peace when we trust God, even in tough times.

When you feel worried or upset, imagine snuggling up in a cozy hammock with Jesus. Tell Him what's bothering you, thank Him for always being with you, and let His peace cover you like a big, soft blanket. Remember, He loves you so much and will help you be brave.

When we have peace in our hearts, we can be peacemakers in our families, friendships, and communities. We can choose to forgive, be kind, and work out problems in a loving way.

One great way to practice peace is by spending quiet time with God each day. Talk to God about your day, read a Bible story, sing a peaceful song, or just sit and listen for His still, small voice. As you soak in His presence, His peace will wash over you like a gentle breeze.

Another way to grow in peace is by memorizing Bible verses about God's peace and promises. When worries start to creep in, say those verses out loud and remind yourself of what's true. One great verse is Isaiah 26:3: "You will keep in perfect peace all who trust in you, all whose thoughts are fixed on you!"

So, let's ask God to fill us with His perfect peace each day, no matter what comes our way. May our lives be like peaceful gardens that bring rest and hope to all who enter.

In this world there is trouble,
but with You there is Peace.
Even in the midst of my mess,
I know you are there with me.

There's Peace for my soul,
mind, and emotions.
You throw all my sins away
as deep as the oceans.

You truly love me,
so with Your Peace I can rest.
All You want from your
children is our very best.

When trouble comes my way,
I can go to sleep at night,
For Your Peace wraps around me,
holding onto me tight.

Patience

Patience means waiting with a happy heart, even when it's hard. Like the avocado at the birthday party – he really wants to eat the yummy cake, but he waits nicely until the birthday song is over and the candles are blown out.

Sometimes waiting is tough, like when we want a turn with a game or a snack from Mom. We might feel like whining or grabbing, but God wants to help us wait patiently and trust His timing.

Did you know God is so patient with us? The Bible says, "The Lord is merciful and compassionate, slow to get angry and filled with unfailing love" (Psalm 145:8). He never gets tired of helping us learn and grow, even when we mess up.

One way to practice patience is to make waiting fun! Sing a song, play "I Spy," or think of something you're excited for. Another way is to remember how patient God is with us and ask Him to help us be patient with others too.

Patience isn't just about waiting, though. It's also about persevering and not giving up when things get hard. Like when we're learning something new, such as a school lesson or riding a bike. It might take a lot of practice and we might feel frustrated at times, but patience helps us keep trying until we get it.

The Bible tells us that patience is important for growing in faith. James 1:3-4 says, "For you know that when your faith is tested, your endurance has a chance to grow. So let it grow, for when your endurance is fully developed, you will be perfect and complete, needing nothing." That means when we patiently trust God through hard times, our faith gets stronger!

Another way to practice patience is by being a good listener. When someone is talking, resist the urge to interrupt or rush them. Instead, wait your turn and show them you care about what they have to say.

So, let's ask God to grow the fruit of
patience in our hearts. As we do, we'll be
living proof of God's goodness and love!

Patience is a fruit
that teaches us to know.
The longer we wait
the more knowledge we will grow.

Ask God for Patience and see
what He will do.
Your blessing is on the way,
coming very soon.

When God is building Patience,
we may think it's a curse.
But trust His timing instead of ours
and stay in His Word.

With Patience comes true
success in any situation.
No matter what happens
you can lead by demonstration.

Kindness

Kindness means doing nice things for others, just because! Like the lemon giving a special gift to the peach, even though the peach wasn't expecting it. When we're kind, it's like sharing a bit of God's love.

The Bible tells us, "Be kind and compassionate to one another, forgiving each other, just as in Christ God forgave you" (Ephesians 4:32). God is so kind to us, even when we don't deserve it. So, He wants us to be kind to others too!

There are lots of fun ways to show kindness – like sharing a toy, making a card for someone who's sad, helping with chores, or telling others about Jesus. Every kind thing we do can make someone's day brighter!

Sometimes, being kind is hard, especially if others aren't kind to us. But we can ask God to help us show His love anyway.

It's not always the big things that make the biggest difference, but the little acts of kindness add up over time. A simple smile, a helping hand, or a word of encouragement can be just what someone needs to feel valued and appreciated.

One great way to practice kindness is to look for ways to serve others. Maybe you could help your little sister clean up her toys or offer to carry groceries for an elderly neighbor. You could also save up your allowance to buy a special treat for a friend or donate to a good cause. As you serve, you'll discover the joy of putting others first and being the hands and feet of Jesus.

Another way to grow in kindness is by choosing to forgive those who hurt you. When someone says or does something mean, it's easy to want to get back at them or hold a grudge. But kindness means letting go of anger and showing mercy, just like God does for us. It's not always easy, but with God's help, we can choose to respond with love and compassion.

So let's make it our mission to be kind today and every day. Let's ask God to give us eyes to see the needs around us and a heart to respond with compassion. May our kindness be a beautiful reflection of our Heavenly Father, who is kind to all He has made (Psalm 145:13).

Kindness is showing someone love even
when they treat you wrong.
To be Kind is to be like Christ
all day long.

Kindness is maturity,
acting with respect.
Turn the other cheek
before putting someone in check.

The act of Kindness is never small,
so continue to pass it on.
The cost is free,
so always answer the call.

Show Kindness to others
who may be going through.
Put a smile on a face that may need it
more than we do.

Goodness

Goodness means choosing to do what's right and kind. See the grape comforting the sad pear? He's showing goodness by being a caring friend.

God is always good to us. The Bible says, "The Lord is good to everyone. He showers compassion on all his creation" (Psalm 145:9). When we follow Jesus, His goodness starts to grow in us like sweet fruit.

One way to show goodness is by obeying God and our parents, even when we don't feel like it. Another way is by being helpful and nice, looking for ways to make life better for others.

Sometimes being good is hard, like when friends want us to do something wrong. But we can ask God to help us be brave and do the right thing. He promises to help us say "no" to bad choices and "yes" to good ones.

Goodness is about being a person of integrity and character, someone who can be trusted to do the right thing, even when no one is looking.

The Bible says, "Fix your thoughts on what is true, and honorable, and right, and pure, and lovely, and admirable. Think about things that are excellent and worthy of praise" (Philippians 4:8). When we focus on these good things, we shape our thoughts and attitudes to be more like Jesus.

Another way to grow in goodness is by hanging out with friends who love God and want to do what's right. Surround yourself with people who bring out the best in you!

We will face challenges and temptations along the way. But God is always with us, ready to help us make good choices.

And when we mess up or make a mistake (because we all do sometimes!), we can always turn back to God and ask for His forgiveness and help to do better next time. He is so patient and kind, and He delights in helping His children grow in goodness.

So today, let's ask God to fill us with His goodness from the inside out. Let's choose to do what's right and kind, even when it's not easy or popular. As we do, we'll be spreading the sweet aroma of Christ everywhere we go! (2 Corinthians 2:15)

Thank You for Your Goodness,
we don't always deserve.
Thank You for Your Son
that You placed on this Earth.

A Savior
who loves, lives, and is real.
To know Goodness
lives is such a big deal.

Thank You for Your Goodness,
for You live inside of me.
You are the lamp unto my light
and a path to my feet.

Faithfulness

Faithfulness means always trusting God and staying close to Him. Like the apple, who starts each day with prayer and Bible study, he's making God his top priority!

We can grow in faithfulness by talking to God every day, learning about Him in the Bible, and doing what He says. When we're faithful in small things, like doing our chores or keeping a promise to a friend, it helps us be faithful in bigger things too.

The Bible is full of people who were faithful to God, even when it was hard. Daniel trusted God and prayed to Him every day, even when a mean king said not to. God kept Daniel safe in a lions' den because of his faithfulness (Daniel 6). Just like Daniel, we can choose to be faithful to God no matter what.

God is always faithful to us. He keeps His promises and never stops loving us, even when we mess up. So let's make being faithful to God our top goal each day!

Faithfulness is a fruit that takes time to grow. The more we practice being faithful in little things, the stronger our faith muscles will become!

Another way to practice faithfulness is by being a reliable and trustworthy friend. When we make a promise, we can do our very best to keep it, even if it's not easy or convenient. We can show up for our friends when they need us, pray for them regularly, and encourage them in their faith. As we prove ourselves faithful in friendship, it will overflow into every other area of our lives.

Sometimes being faithful means standing strong for what we believe in, even when others don't understand or agree. It can be scary to be different or go against the crowd, but we can trust that God is with us and will give us the courage we need.

So, let's make it our mission to be faithful friends of God. Let's talk to Him often, trust Him completely, and follow Him wherever He leads. And let's watch in amazement as He grows a beautiful harvest of faithfulness in us and through us, for His glory and our good!

You are loving, loyal, and Faithful.
The God who never fails.
Your Faithfulness is shown every day
By Your Son who was nailed.

Oh, how much I love You,
because You chose me before I knew,
Your Faithfulness is so heartwarming
that I know now what to do.

Show Faithfulness to others,
like what Christ has done for me,
I can show that to the world
and they'll start to believe.

To bring more to the Kingdom
is the plan all along,
But it starts with Faithfulness
and Love for others to be drawn.

Gentleness

Gentleness means being tender and loving in how we treat others. The blueberry is gently helping the orange who fell, even though the orange was mean before. The blueberry is responding with kindness instead of meanness.

Jesus was always gentle, even with those who hurt Him. He invites us to be gentle too, saying, "Blessed are the meek" (Matthew 5:5). It's not about being weak or letting others walk all over us, but about having the strength and self-control to respond with love and grace, even in tough situations.

We can practice gentleness by using nice words, even when we're upset. Instead of yelling or saying something mean, we can take a deep breath, pray, and choose to speak kindly. Gentleness is like a soft pillow that makes others feel safe and accepted.

One way to practice gentleness is by being a good listener. When someone is sharing their thoughts or feelings with us, we can give them our full attention and show them we care. Instead of interrupting or trying to fix their problems, we can simply offer a listening ear and a caring heart.

Another way to grow in gentleness is to be careful and considerate with our words. The Bible says, "A gentle answer deflects anger, but harsh words make tempers flare" (Proverbs 15:1). When we speak with kindness and respect, even when we disagree with someone, it can diffuse tension and create a more peaceful atmosphere.

Gentleness also means being humble and putting others first instead of always insisting on our own way or trying to prove we're right. We can look for ways to serve and support others.

Of course, being gentle doesn't mean never standing up for what's right. Sometimes, the most loving and gentle thing we can do is speak the truth, even when it's hard to hear. But we can do it with a heart of compassion and a desire to help, not hurt.

Let's be quick to listen, slow to speak, and always ready to respond with love. And let's watch in wonder as He uses our gentle words and actions to bring healing, hope, and grace to all we meet.

Gentleness is the thing
that is kind, a soft touch.
It's not always in the world,
but is it too much?

Thank You for Gentleness
for I can be kind.
I want to think like You
and keep You on my mind.

Gentleness is a fruit
that needs to be shown.
Instead of showing hatred
and anger, the social norm.

His Glory reigns
and His presence is near,
To be Gentle and kind,
the One who cheers.

Self-Control

Self-control means choosing to do what's right, even when we really want to do something else. Like the watermelon in the story who had no money — he found the plum's dollar and wanted to buy ice cream with it, but instead, he returned it to the plum. That's self-control in action!

Sometimes it's hard to make good choices. When we ask Him for help, He gives us the power to say "no" to bad things and "yes" to good things.

One way to practice self-control is by pausing and praying before we act, especially when we're feeling a big emotion like anger or sadness. We can ask God to help us make a wise choice that honors Him.

Practice self-control by managing your time wisely. When we're tempted to waste time or procrastinate, we can ask God to help us stay focused and use our time in a way that honors Him.

Another way to grow in self-control is by being careful about what we let into our minds and hearts. The Bible says, "Guard your heart above all else, for it determines the course of your life" (Proverbs 4:23). That means we should be thoughtful about the movies and TV shows we watch, the music we listen to, and the books we read. We can avoid things that could lead us away from God.

Self-control also means being disciplined in taking care of our bodies, which are temples of the Holy Spirit (1 Corinthians 6:19). We can practice self-control by eating healthy foods, getting enough sleep and exercise, and avoiding things that could harm us, like drugs or too much junk food.

We don't have to rely on our own willpower alone. We can say, like Paul, "For I can do everything through Christ, who gives me strength" (Philippians 4:13).

Ask God to help you make wise decisions that honor Him. Let's surround ourselves with friends and activities that encourage us to live for Jesus.

The world often tells us to do whatever feels good in the moment. We'll show others that there is a better way that comes from following Jesus.

Self-Control is between
Spirit and flesh.
One is about life
and the other is about death.

Self-Control helps teach
the way of life.
But sometimes the wrong choice
can cost you a price.

So who will you let control you?
The King?
Or the enemy
and the lies he will bring.

The enemy kills, steals,
and destroys (John 10:10).
That is all a part of his plan.
So pick Spirit over flesh
and follow the Lord's commands.

Conclusion

We've learned so much about the fruit of the Spirit – love, joy, peace, patience, kindness, goodness, faithfulness, gentleness, and self-control. When we stay connected to Jesus, He helps us grow these beautiful qualities in our hearts.

Of course, growing takes time. There will be days when we mess up or feel like we're not growing at all. But that's okay! God is so patient and faithful. He promises to forgive us and to keep helping us as we trust and obey Him. It's not about trying harder or being perfect but about staying close to Jesus and letting Him change us from the inside out.

So, let's keep walking with Jesus each day – talking to Him, learning from the Bible, and looking for ways to practice the fruit of the Spirit. And let's thank God every time we see Him working in us and through us.

And as we do, we'll be a beautiful garden that brings glory to God and draws others to Him. People will see the light and love of Jesus shining through us, and they'll want to experience it for themselves.

Always remember, my friend, that you are deeply loved by God. He created you; He chose you, and He has an incredible plan for your life. No matter what happens, you can trust that He is with you, He is for you, and He will never stop helping you.

You are a masterpiece in the making, a work of art that God is crafting day by day. And as you let Him mold you and shape you, you'll become all that He created you to be – a shining light that points the way to Him. Let's pray:

Dear Jesus,

Thank You so much for the gift of Your Spirit living in us. We know that we can't grow these things on our own, but we trust that You will help us every step of the way. Fill us with Your Spirit today. Help us stay connected to Your love and power. Give us the strength to make wise choices and the courage to be kind and loving. Use us to make a difference in the world for You. May our lives be a beautiful garden that brings glory to Your name and draws others to You. Thank You for Your faithfulness and patience with us. We know that You will keep molding us and shaping us into the masterpiece You created us to be. We trust You and we love You. In Jesus' name we pray, amen.

"But the Holy Spirit produces this kind of fruit in our lives: love, joy, peace, patience, kindness, goodness, faithfulness, gentleness, and self-control. There is no law against these things!" (Galatians 5:22-23)

Dedication

To my phenomenal wife Milagros, my steadfast partner on this faith journey. You spoke life into my dreams and awakened the writer within me. Your unwavering prayers and heartfelt encouragement have been my anchor. Thank you for your "Yes" to God. I love you more than words can express.

I dedicate this book to my beloved daughter, Mariah Gianna Ford, the delight of my soul. As you were being formed in Mama's tummy, God planted the seed of this book within me. May these pages reveal to you the power of the Holy Spirit and the depths of Jesus' love—a love that surpasses even mine. For He is your Rock, your Refuge, and Your Strong Tower.

As you grow, I pray that you will display these truths at home with your precious baby brother Micah and everyone in your life. May the Good News of Christ flow from your lips, touching lives with the love and truth you've discovered in these pages.

Daddy loves you boundlessly. You all are my pride, my joy, and my greatest blessing. May this book be a lasting reminder of the incredible journey we're on together as a family, growing in faith and love.

About the Author

Marcus J. Ford, a native of Southern California, graduated from Centennial High School in Corona, CA. With a heart for making a positive impact on young lives, Marcus works as a Behavior Coach at a local elementary school, where he dedicates his time to guiding and nurturing students. Additionally, he serves as a basketball trainer, combining his love for the sport with his desire to mentor and inspire youth.

With a passion for personal and spiritual development, Marcus enjoys playing basketball, working out, and immersing himself in studying the Bible during his free time. Driven by a deep sense of purpose, Marcus aspires to write more books that help children understand their identity in Christ and experience the transformative power of Jesus' love. Through his

writing, he aims to equip the next generation with the tools they need to cultivate strong faith and live a life rooted in the unwavering love of God.

A devoted husband to his wife Milagros and a loving father to their children, Marcus finds great joy in family life. Together with their beloved dog Bing, the Ford family resides in Broken Arrow, Oklahoma.

www.ingramcontent.com/pod-product-compliance
Lightning Source LLC
Chambersburg PA
CBHW051210090426
42740CB00021B/3447